MINI-GUIDES

ARMOR IN NORMANDY: THE BRITISH..........

June - August 1944

by Alexandre THERS

Lay-out by the author - Computer drawings by Antoine POGGIOLI
Translated from the French by Jonathan NORTH

h&c
PARIS

BRITISH ARMORED FORCES IN 1944

Those British armored units which disembarked in Normandy benefited from a high degree of logistical and doctrinal sophistication. Much of this had been gained from the disastrous experience of the Dieppe landings in 1942. In this section we will examine the British organization, the equipment used in their divisions and their combat capability.

BRITISH ARMORED DIVISIONS IN 1944

British armored divisions were based on an organization established in 1942. This had seen the replacement of one of the division's armored brigades with a brigade of infantry and by a substantial increase in divisional artillery. But the British were facing something of a crisis. They had reached a plateau in their resources and found that their expansion was now limited by lack of personnel and an inability to maintain their effectives. The most recently formed division was the 79th, established in 1942. In 1943 an initiative to boost the ranks of the infantry saw the transfer away of personnel from the Royal Armoured Corps to the infantry. The role of the armored unit, whilst still seen as vital, was somewhat marginalized and official doctrine would now emphasize that armored units were to be used to exploit breakthroughs. The bulk of British armor therefore found itself as infantry support and it should be emphasized that only the British made the distinction between assault tanks and infantry tanks. Such a rigid and inflexible system made the British unique among the belligerents.

The received opinion was that tanks acting in support of infantry required effective armor more than they needed firepower or speed. Despite this theory, British armored divisions did receive a boost to their firepower when, in 1943, they began to receive American Shermans which, along with the British Churchill IV and Cromwell IV, could fire more effective anti-tank and explosive shells.

A British armored division was composed of armored brigades. These were rather like German panzer regiments but with the difference that they were more frequently employed as independent units and could call upon a greater number of vehicles. There were 190 medium tanks and 33 light tanks in a British brigade and 160 medium and heavy in a Panzer regiment. The British brigade was composed of three tank regiments. An armored division had one such armored brigade as well as a Motor Battalion of mechanized infantry on half-tracks and an infantry brigade riding in trucks. A fourth armored regiment, along with a further battalion of infantry, made up the unit's Armoured Reconnaissance Regiment. Reconnaissance was carried out by these troops but could also be accomplished by detaching this unit from the armored division and using it at corps level. The divisional artillery was composed of two motorized artillery regiments, an anti-tank regiment and an anti-aircraft regiment.

A British armored division had a theoretical strength of 244 light or medium tanks, 25 anti-aircraft vehicles and 8 command tanks. This made it numerically stronger than its German equivalent even though, in terms of firepower, their adversaries had the edge.

OTHER ARMORED UNITS

There were three further types of formation in the British Army in addition to armored divisions and brigades. These were the Army or Corps Reserve, the corps reconnaissance units and the reconnaissance regiments attached to infantry divisions. All these were drawn from the Royal Armoured Corps.

Reconnaissance regiments performed long-range missions in order to probe enemy defense and discover enemy intentions. They were attached to the staff of each of the four Army Corps engaged in Normandy. Such units relied primarily on armored cars and half-tracks.

Independent armored brigades were used to form a Corps Reserve, a general reserve used to support infantry formations. Such units relied primarily on Shermans and Churchills. They were designated Type A if they included a battalion of mechanized infantry and Type B if they did not.

The Royal Armoured Corps itself was formed from a variety of units. There were those whose origins lay in the British cavalry, the Royal Tank Regiment, which was organized into tank battalions, and the Yeomanry which was composed of armored regiments from the Territorial Army. Then there were tank regiments formed from personnel transferred from the infantry. There were also Armoured

Delivery Squadrons, acting as transport units or for supplying personnel or equipment. There were also the Great Headquarter Liaison Regiments (or Phantom units) used to keep HQ informed of the movement of Allied troops and their exact dispositions.

EQUIPMENT

Armored vehicles employed in Normandy can be divided into five distinct types:

Medium Tanks

The British did not have a heavy tank as such but used medium tanks equipped with 75 mm or 76.2 mm guns on traversing turrets. They were designed to be as flexible as possible, to engage enemy tanks, should occasion require, or to act against enemy positions of all types.

Infantry Tanks

These were capable of destroying mines and acting against nearly all kinds of German fortified positions.

Amphibious Tanks

These were supposed to make their own way to the shore and then act as supports for the first waves of infantry while they secured the landing beaches.

Specialist Vehicles

These tanks would play a crucial role not only during the actual landings but also one equally important in the delicate phase between the landing and the push into the interior.

Tank Destroyers

These were designed to intervene to destroy enemy armor should it be encountered, allowing tanks to concentrate on exploiting any breakthrough.

In general British equipment had certain qualities but also some intrinsic weaknesses. British assault tanks were, for example, inferior to their German counterparts. The Cromwell and the Sherman, an American tank, formed the backbone of the British armored force. Appearing in mid-1942 and January 1943 respectively, these tanks were surpassed by their German equivalents. This was particularly true in terms of armor and armament, the German Panther and Tiger I and IIs being much superior. Nevertheless, British tanks proved themselves worthy opponents to the Panzer IV and the equals of the StuG III and IV assault guns, particularly as the latter suffered from a lack of mobility and from unreliability.

It was the arrival of the Sherman Firefly with its 76.2 mm gun, which lifted the morale of the British tank crews as well as the introduction of the effective APDS (Armor Piercing Discarding Sabot) projectile. Even so, in terms of armor,

superior German tactics and the use the Germans made of the terrain - which was very much in the favor of those defending Normandy - British tanks were vulnerable. Only the Churchill, based on an old-fashioned design, boasted effective armor. But it is out-classed by their adversaries in the other domains. Despite this qualitative difference, the British at least had a numerical superiority, a constant flow of supplies and rapid replacement of destroyed or damaged vehicles in their favor.

THE CONTEXT

Although Normandy was selected as the destination for a massive Allied invasion, which would rely, in good measure, on armored units, it was in fact a region ill suited for the deployment of armored forces. To the east, around the Orne estuary, the British found themselves confronted by a well-defended coast dotted with German strongholds. The area behind the coast was dominated by the major towns of Bayeux, Caen and Falaise and these were linked by main roads. Consequently, after the actual landings had succeeded, one of the key objectives of the campaign would be the seizure of these communication hubs. These would provide suitable bases from which the Allies could venture out and provoke the Germans into open battle.

This elaborate scheme depended entirely on the successful seizure of the actual landing beaches. This was done thanks, in part, to specialist armored vehicles. From then on Allied tactics were largely dictated by the terrain. Only the plain to the south of Caen provided a suitable arena for large-scale armored actions. Everywhere else, especially when the Germans could maintain themselves in the bocage, the advantage lay with the defenders. British doctrine, in contrast to that adopted by the Americans, proved itself rigid and conventional. Tanks would often attack alone, rarely supported by infantry, and, as a result, suffered heavy casualties. This was the case in Operation Goodwood. On the other hand the British benefited from the cooperation between tanks and aircraft whilst the Germans saw little of the exhausted Luftwaffe. Finally, although the deployment of British armor was outmoded, it did at least prevent German panzer divisions around Caen from seizing the initiative.

With the exception of Goodwood, British tanks were used parsimoniously, despite it being, on paper, the most imposing Allied armored force. In all five armored divisions and eight independent brigades (Including Canadian and Polish units) were available. That meant some 3,300 Sherman, Churchill and Cromwell tanks as well as important reserves.

THE DUPLEX DRIVE 'SHERMAN'

Perhaps the most unusual Sherman variant was the amphibious Duplex Drive (DD) based on the Mk II or the Mk V.

*A*n excellent view of the twin propellers fixed in position and connected to their drive axles. (IWM)

....

*B*ottom: ADD with its skirt deflated. British landings at Gold, Juno and Sword were made, with rare exceptions, in good conditions. (IWM)

....

*B*elow: intercom switch box for the No. 19 wireless set. If the tank driver wished to call the tank's commander he simply pressed the button and spoke.
(Van Onsem Collection)

The tank was fitted with a flotation skirt constructed out of 36 tubes. These allowed the tank to actually float. It could be launched from a boat and could traverse a relatively short distance to the coast. Twin propellers connected to the tank's motor guaranteed the tank a speed of 6 km an hour over a calm sea. The propellers could be operated while the skirt was inflated by means of a lever that was connected to the propellers through a series of rods. The actual term Duplex Drive stems from the mechanical transmission which meant that the engine could switch from powering the twin propellers to powering the sprocket wheels. The tank's flotation skirt meant that the tank could float to the shore; once there, the skirt was deflated and the tank's engine reverted to acting as a normal tank's engine. One of the advantages of the DD was that the front of the inflatable skirt could be lowered to allow the tank to make use of its gun, even while it was still in the water.

The tank's interior was replete with all the usual equipment — engine, transmission, weapons, ammunition and equipment — but also contained hydraulic pumps and the controls to operate the skirt and the propellers. Among all the special equipment should be mentioned the electronic pumps which jettisoned water from the tank by means of compressed air. All this extra

The Duplex Drive Sherman evolved from a British concept. The skirt would be kept rigid by the 36 inflatable tubes but also by foldable metal rods. (Illustration by Jean Restayn)

TECHNICAL DATA

Crew: 5
Combat weight: 30.3 tons
Engine: Continental R975 C1, 9-cylinder gasoline engine, 400 hp
Max. speed on road: 34 km/h
Range on road: 193 km
Fuel capacity: 796 liters
Armament: 1 x 75 mm M3 gun, 2 x 7.62 mm M1919 A4 machineguns, 1 x 12.7 mm M2HB anti-aircraft machinegun
Ammunition: 97 shells, 5,050 mg rounds
Armor thickness (max. without mantlet): 51 mm at 56°
Radio: No. 19

*R*ight: the lamp used on board the Sherman was the Lamp, Operator No. 6. (Van Onsem Collection)

....

*O*pposite: during exercises on a calm sea the DD was relatively maneuverable. Because of its weight its fee board was around 30 cm. (IWM)

machinery seriously reduced the amount of space within the tank. At the time the DD was classified as a secret weapon and when crews were formed and trained in March 1944, one of the first things with which they were familiarized with was the tank's respiratory equipment, which was so vast that it considerably reduced the chance of getting out of the escape hatches. Nearly 100 such tanks were used on D-Day by the British and Americans.

THE 'SHERMAN'

This American medium tank was the mainstay of the US and British armored forces and it was probably manufactured more than any other. The British used the Mk I (M4), Mk II (M4A1), Mk III (M4A2) and Mk V (M4A4).

A M4A4 (or Mark V in British terminology) Sherman belonging the 4th Canadian Armored Division. This photograph was taken on August 8, 1944. The standard anti-tank shell used with the 75 mm M3 was the M61 armor piercing shell, which could pierce 68 mm armor from a range of 450 m and 60 mm from 900m. (K. Bell, NACPA, 131373)

....

B ottom right: a Sleeve insignia as worn by men of the 11th Armoured Division. (Militaria Magazine)

....

B elow: a column of Sherman Mk IIIs (M4A2) of the 11th Armoured Division await the launch of Operation Goodwood. The radio antennae suggest the first tank is a command vehicle. (IWM)

It was a simple design, robust, reliable, fast and easy to maintain. All this made it extremely popular among tank crews and mechanics. It had other advantages too, including the excellent Wright Continental engine (although the M4A3 was provided with a Ford V8) and an automatic gearbox and transmission. On the wet version, ammunition was enclosed in cases lined with glycerin and water which reduced the risk of fire should the tank be hit. It also had an excellent intercom system for communication and a turret which could rotate 360 degrees and housed a gun, which is gyrostabilized in elevation.

This ability to rotate made it superior to similar German tanks, but the tank's rate of fire was also faster (20 rounds a minute). The Sherman could also be fitted with a variety of tracks to cross different types of terrain. Its chief weapon was the 75 mm gun with a maximum range of 3000 meters although this was reduced by half when firing penetration rounds.

These rounds did not achieve sufficient velocity at close range making it extremely difficult for the Shermans to be effective at close range against German heavy tanks. Although outgunned by the Panther, the M4 compensated with its numerical superiority and its reliability, but the tank suffered

TECHNICAL DATA
(Mark I and II, hybrid)
Crew: 5
Combat weight: 30.3 tons
Engine: Continental R975 C1, 9-cylinder gasoline engine, 400 hp
Max. speed on road: 39 km/h
Range on road: 193 km
Fuel capacity: 796 liters
Length: 5.89 m
Width: 2.62 m
Height: 2.74 m
Armament: 1 x 75 mm M3 gun, 2 x 7.62 mm M1919 A4 machine guns, 1 x 12.7 mm M2HB anti-aircraft machinegun
Ammunition: 97 shells, 5,050 MG rounds
Armor thickness (max. without mantlet): 51 mm at 56°
Radio: No. 19

*R*ight: the base of the antennae belonging to a wireless set No. 19 (post B). (Van Onsem Collection)

*O*pposite: Sherman Vs and Vcs belonging to the 4th Canadian Armoured Division speed towards Falaise. Sherman mobility was excellent on a road but relatively poor on rougher terrain. (K. Bell, NACPA, 140822)

A Sherman Flail tank. American reluctance to demote the Sherman and replace it with a heavy tank stemmed from what was essentially a logistical problem. American tanks had to be transported by sea to Europe or to the Pacific and a heavy tank would reduce the amount of other essential equipment a ship could carry. (Illustration by Jean Restayn)

from poor armor and from the propensity to brew up when hit.

The British converted the Sherman into a number of variants, each designed to perform a specific role; there was the BARV (Beach Armoured Recovery Vehicle), designed to rescue to recover vehicles and tanks from the invasion beach (its turret was removed and a jib and haulage gear added to tow vehicles); the Crab or Flail had a revolving drum of chains fitted to clear mines.

The tank marked its path through a minefield by depositing chalk along its route. The ARV, or Sherman Armoured Recovery Vehicle, also had its turret removed and an A-frame jib added. The ARV Mk II was even provided with a dummy gun. Other variants also went into action, not least the Duplex Drive and the Fascine Roller.

THE 'SHERMAN' FIREFLY

In order to have a chance of taking on German heavy tanks with any hope of success, the British decided that they should attempt to modify the Sherman. They therefore mounted their redoubtable 17-pounder gun and gave the resulting variant the nickname of Firefly.

In fact there were three basic versions - the Mk IIc, based on an M4's hybrid hull; the Mk Ic, based on the M4's hull (both versions were driven by a Continental motor); and the Mk Vc, the most effective version, utilizing a Chrysler Multibank engine. The British decision to replace the American 75 mm gun with their own 17-pounder, complete with muzzle break, was taken in 1943. In fact, the weapon was largely superior to the American 75 mm and 76.2 mm and gave the tank a firepower equal to that of the Panther. But mounting such a gun called for a serious revision of the tank's superstructure. Counterweights had to be added, the turret elongated towards the back to absorb the gun's recoil and a more powerful engine had to be utilized. Nevertheless British crews now had a chance of success should they encounter a Panther or Tiger. The only problem was that the level of protection afforded by the Firefly's armor was inferior. By February 1944 the conversion of Sherman chassis to the new design began in earnest so that the greatest possible number of Fireflys would be ready for the Normandy landings. The Firefly was by far the best tank deployed by the Allies in Normandy. There was one Firefly to four Shermans or Cromwells in each platoon.

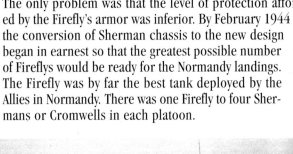

British firepower was considerably augmented by the simultaneous adoption of the 17-pounder and the APDS (Armor Piercing Discarding Sabot) projectile. (IWM B8793)

Below: spare valves belonging to a wireless set No. 19. (Van Onsem Collection)

TECHNICAL DATA

Crew: 5
Combat weight: 32.7 tons
Engine: Chrysler Multibank
A57, 30-cylinder gasoline
engine, 425 hp
Max. speed on road:
40 km/h
Range on road: 161 km
Fuel capacity: 727 liters
Length with gun: 7.85 m
Length without gun: 6.45 m
Width: 2.67 m
Height: 2.74 m
Armament: 1 x ROQF 17-
pounder (7.62 mm) Mk IV or
VII gun, 1 x 7.62 mm M1919
A4 machinegun
Ammunition: 77 shells,
5,000 MG rounds
**Armor thickness (max.
without mantlet):** 76 mm
Radio: No. 19

*P**receding page: a 17-pounder's
penetrating round.
(Private Collection)*

*P**receding page and opposite:
the outline of the Mk Vc
is shown here during operations.
Note the distinctive design
of the British tracks. (IWM)*

*A Firefly's cupola, positioned on the turret, allowed a quick exit from the tank
in case of an emergency. It also meant that the tank commander had excellent
visibility. (Illustration by Jean Restayn) Below: a receiver/transmitter from
a wireless set No. 19. (Van Onsem Collection)*

THE MKV (M3A3) 'STUART' LIGHT TANK

A rear view of a Stuart. Mudguards were rarely used in combat. (Tank Museum, 2739/C3)

B elow: a variometer Mk III which connected the antennae to the speaker of a wireless set No. 19. (Van Onsem Collection)

This diminutive American tank was the last in the line of M3s and differed from its predecessor in among other things, its modified chassis. By the end of 1943 it was generally considered by the Americans to be out of date and they were switching to the M5A1. Nevertheless, the British believed the tank was still useful as a reconnaissance vehicle.

For that reason the Stuart was the standard light tank issued to armored brigade reconnaissance units. Produced in vast quantities it was highly regarded by crews. They liked its reliability, the ease with which it was maintained, its mobility (it had a great weight to power ratio), its excellent acceleration and its speed. Indeed it was one of the fastest tanks of the war.

The interior of the tank was well designed. It was padded with rubber, insulating the crew and increasing their protection as they sat on specially designed seats within the cabin. Gaps between the armor plating were sealed to increase noise reduction levels. Communications were assured by the use of intercoms, speakers and laryngophones.

The tank's 37 mm gun, an M5 or M6, was fitted with a gyrostabilizer and this gave it great precision even when the tank was mobile. Just like the Sherman, the Stuart had a choice of track and could select rubber or metal according to the terrain. The hull was welded with the exception of the transmission block that was bolted on to the glacis.

B ottom right: despite a number of improvements, making the Stuart V a superior tank to any of its predecessors, it was still nothing more than a transitional vehicle. (Tank Museum, 2739/C4)

I nsignia of the 49th Reconnaissance regiment. It belonging to the Reconnaissance Corps, a part of the Royal Armoured Corps. (Militaria Magazine)

TECHNICAL DATA

Crew: 4
Combat weight: 14.7 tons
Engine: Continental W-670-9A, 7-cylinder gasoline engine, 262 hp; or a Guiberson T1020, 9-cylinder gasoline engine, 242 hp
Max. speed on road: 57 km/h
Max. speed across country: 32 km/h
Range on road: 217 km
Fuel capacity: 500 liters
Length: 5.03 m
Width: 2.52 m
Height: 2.57 m
Armament: 1 x 37 mm M6 gun, 3 x 7.62 mm M1919 A4 machineguns
Ammunition: 174 shells, 7,500 MG rounds
Armor thickness (max. without mantlet): 44 mm
Radio: No. 19

*O*pposite: although ill-equipped for combat missions, the Stuart was still common and each British armored regiment was equipped with 11 such tanks. (Tank Museum 2739/B2)

*T*he Stuart M3A3 had ample room in its rear for the storage of equipment. This was augmented by the addition of a metal box fixed to the back of the tank. (Illustration by Jean Restayn)

Despite its qualities the tank suffered from distinct limitations. Its armament was out-of-date and completely ineffective against German armor. It couldn't even fire explosive shells. Its silhouette was high, its armor weak (51 mm on the mantlet) and its tracks too thin to cope with rough terrain.

*O*pposite: a shoulder flash as adopted in June 1943 and worn by personnel of the Reconnaissance Corps. (Militaria Magazine)

THE MARK VII 'TETRARCH'

This small, light tank was developed in 1938. At first it was known as the Purdah but was renamed the Tetrarch in 1943. It was completely obsolete by 1944 but continued in service. Its light weight, for example, allowed it to be adapted for use by airborne forces. It was even transported by Hamilcar gliders, especially designed for that purpose.

*T*his Tetrarch belongs to the British 6th Airborne Division and carries a supplementary fuel tank. (Bovington Tank Museum)

*B*elow: an Enfield Commando revolver of the type popular amongst tank crews and mechanized troops. (Private Collection)

The Tetrarch was armed with a 40 mm gun, which made it completely incapable of defending itself against enemy tanks. Its hull had armor that was only between 4 mm and 14 mm thick, offering the crew the most illusory protection. The driver's visibility could be much improved by opening a rectangular vision slit. There was no cupola for the commander in the turret but smoke dischargers were fitted on either side. The driving mechanism was different too: the driving sprocket was the same size as the wheels but was placed behind them. The tank was steered rather like a car. The front wheels could pivot, flexing the tracks, and the tank could thus be turned in either direction. The tracks were removable allowing the tank to move at speed along roads. Indeed

The British military refused to have anything to do with the Mk VII Tetrach, and only 177 examples were produced. (Illustration by Jean Restayn)

one of the few advantages of this mini-tank was its speed which allowed it to scamper away from any chance encounter with a superior enemy. Designed to support infantry it was employed, along with Universal Carriers, by 6th Airborne around Ranville. Their role was relatively insignificant and they were soon replaced by Cromwells.

Opposite: sleeve insignia as worn by men of the 6th Airborne Division. (Militaria Magazine)

Preceding page: this photo, which shows a Tetrarch backing into a Hamilcar glider, gives a good idea of the size of the tank. (Bovington Tank Museum)

Opposite: this photo gives a good idea as to the unique way in which the Tetrarch's turret hatch opened. (Bovington Tank Museum)

THE 'CHURCHILL'

Examples of this medium infantry tank first appeared in 1941, but following a number of modifications, it remained in service until 1944. The Mark IV, VI and VII were most frequently encountered in Normandy.

T his photo reveals the powerful stature of a Churchill tank. (IWM)

Its turret, cast out of steel, mounted a 75 mm gun with a muzzle break and this allowed the tank to fire both penetrative and explosive shells. The Churchill owed its longevity to the following chracteristics: its tracks were partly concealed but the tank had a unique steering mechanism. The driver, using hydraulic steering and clutch controls, could turn the tank 90 degrees even when the tank was immobile. The engine itself was very dependable; it had good stability and was reliable but very slow. The tank's main advantage was the thickness of its armor, which varied from 90 mm to 152 mm. The Mark VII, which appeared in 1944, used a modified turret and chassis.

B elow: a tank commander's Tannoy microphone. (Van Onsem Collection)

The Churchill produced a number of variants and many of these were employed in Normandy. There was the Small Box Girder which could lay a small pontoon bridge; the Bridgelayer, which could lay a flexible metal bridge across ditches or over anti-tank obstacles; the Crocodile, equipped with a flame-thrower with a range of 110 meters and 1 800 liters of flammable liquid; the AVRE (Armoured Vehicle, Royal Engineers), which mounted

TECHNICAL DATA
(Mark IV)

Crew: 5
Combat weight: 39.6 tons
Engine: 2 x Bedford Twin-Six, 6-cylinder gasoline engine, 350 hp
Max. speed on road: 25 km/h
Max. speed across country: 13 km/h
Range on road: 259 km
Range across country: 154 km
Fuel capacity: 682 liters (plus 148 liters in reserve fuel tanks)
Length: 7.35 m
Width: 3.25 m
Height: 2.45 m
Armament: 1 x 6 pounder (75 mm) gun, 2 x 7.92 mm Besa machineguns, 1 x 7.92 mm Bren machinegun
Ammunition: 84 shells, 7,525 MG rounds
Armor thickness (max.): 101 mm
Radio: No. 19

Preceding page: the Churchill only served with the 79th Armoured Division and independent tank brigades (such as the Guards, the 31st and the 34th. (IWM, B 9162)

The Churchill's armament (as shown here on this Mark VII) was too weak, like that of most British tanks, and this severely affected the morale of British tank crews. (Illustration by Jean Restayn)

a Mk III Petard 290 mm mortar in the turret, ideal for destroying blockhouses and finally, there were Churchills converted into towing units and the AVRE with Log Carpet Device, a unit designed to lay a carpet of logs over trenches and ditches.

Opposite: a monkey wrench as used onboard a Churchill. (F. Bachmann Collection)

Below: a Churchill AVRE equipped with a special bridging unit to enable troops to cross marshy ground. (Bovington Tank Museum)

THE 'CROMWELL' MARK IV

For the British, the Cromwell represented an important step forward in the evolution of their medium tanks. Although it was perhaps inferior in firepower to German tanks in this category, despite its new 75 mm Mark V gun, it made up for that with its greater mobility.

A Cromwell IV belonging to the staff of the 11th Armoured Division trundles through Normandy. Like the Sherman, the Cromwell's gunner could rely on a number of aides and sights for direct or indirect fire. (IWM)

Below: a radio set such as this was carried by a number of British tanks. (F. Bachmann Collection)

It was the first British tank to be built with a reliable and powerful engine, one adapted from the Rolls Royce Merlin. This, combined with an excellent track mechanism, allowed the tank to attain speeds of 52 km an hour on the road. The tank also had an efficient gearbox. As with most British tanks the armor was riveted together and was relatively square, but it was also rather weak because the thickness of its frontal armor at 75 mm, was much less than that of its principal adversaries, the Panzer IV, Panther and Tiger. The turret, which housed the commander, gunner and loader (who also acted as radio operator), was designed so that additional armor could be bolted on. The turret could be rotated 360 degrees in just 15 seconds thanks to its excellent hydraulics. The Mark IV was riveted together whilst the Mark V and VII were welded. The tank's gun could fire penetrating and explosive rounds, many of the shells being American Lend-lease. The replacement of the gun by a 17-pounder, capable of penetrating a German Tiger's armor, was considered at one stage, but

Below: this Cromwell VIII, armed with a 95 mm howitzer, would be used to support infantry. (IWM)

*T*he Cromwell's 75 mm gun and its Besa machine gun could be fired by means of a special pedal.
(Illustration by Jean Restayn)

TECHNICAL DATA

Crew: 5
Combat weight: 28 tons
Engine: Rolls Royce Meteor, V 12
cylinder gasoline engine, 600 hp
Max. speed on road: 52 km/h
Max. speed across country:
29 km/h
Range on road: 265 km
Range across country:
180 km
Fuel capacity: 527 liters
Length: 6.35 m
Width: 2.91 m
Height: 2.49 m
Armament: 1 x 75 mm ROQF
MKV or VA gun, 2 x 7.92 mm
Besa machineguns
Ammunition: 64 shells, 4,950
MG rounds
Armor thickness (max.): 76 mm
Radio: No. 19

*R*ight: a manual for the wireless
set No. 19 as published
by the Canadian Department
of National Defence.
(Van Onsem Collection)

*O*pposite: Cromwells gather
on the plains between Caen
and Falaise in August 1944.
(IWM B8835)

because of the shortness of the hull the idea was discarded.

The Cromwell was popular with the famous 7th Armoured Division as well as with reconnaissance regiments belonging to other divisions. A variant, the Centaur, identical but for its out-of-date Liberty engine, also served in Europe. Some 80 tanks were adapted to take a 95 mm howitzer and many of these were used during D-Day. Most Centaurs were later converted to Cromwell variants, often being fashioned into specialist vehicles (towing units, bulldozers, anti-aircraft units or observation platforms). The Cromwell's chassis served as the basis for the Challenger which, with its lengthened hull, could mount a 17-pdr. These were issued to units, which had not yet received the Firefly in order to give them some heavy support.

THE 'ACHILLES' TANK DESTROYER IIc

This was the British version of the American M10 and it mounted a British 17-pounder. Only the turret, with its open-top, and the chassis structure, have a new design.

This metal case contained the daily rations for two soldiers. (Van Onsem Collection)

....

Below: two versions of the Achilles were eventually built. Version I, equipped with an American M1, and version IIc with the 17-pounder gun, counterweights and the form of turret eventually adopted. The brackets for the mounting of additional armor did not appear on the final version. (IWM)

With the Achilles the British at last found a vehicle that was capable of beating enemy tanks and providing heavy support for infantry. The basis of the vehicle was the American M4A2 or M4A3 with modified superstructures and heavier weaponry. The Achilles was lightly armored on its glacis plate and along its flanks but this could be overcome by bolting on additional armor making it possible for the vehicle to serve as an assault tank. In reality, additional armor was rarely used as this significantly increased the strain on the engine and affected the vehicle's performance. The turret was relatively cramped, the rear and sides being further reduced by the slope of the armor, a design supposed to deflect enemy shells. However the thin armor offered little by way of protection to the crew and the open-top rendered them relatively vulnerable to mortar fire or grenades. The IIc carried a 17-pounder, which, like its American counterpart, gave it excellent firepower but required a complete overhaul of the turret.

The Achilles carried 50 shells and 44 of them these were stored in the rear of the hull, only 6 being housed in the turret. (Illustration by Jean Restayn)

TECHNICAL DATA

Crew: 5
Combat weight: 29.6 tons
Engine: GM 6046, 6-cylinder diesel engine, 375 hp
Max. speed on road: 40 km/h
Range on road: 322 km
Fuel capacity: 750 liters
Length without gun: 5.97 m
Length with gun: 7.27 m
Width: 3.05 m
Height: 2.90 m
Armament: 1 x 17-pounder Mk V gun, 1 x 12.7 mm Browning
Ammunition: 50 shells, 450 MG rounds
Armor thickness (max. without mantlet): 51 mm
Radio: No. 19

Opposite: an Achilles abandoned somewhere along the road between Caen and Falaise. It belonged to a Canadian unit. (Tank Museum 3000/B4)

Right: this little bag contained a number of elements for fixing a wireless set No. 19 in place. The designation Philu - 43 suggests that these components were manufactured in the USA. (Van Onsem Collection)

Other significant differences were the muzzle break and the counterweights built in to compensate for the weight of the gun barrel and reduce recoil. The tank, with its low silhouette, used a diesel engine and carried 50 shells. Highly mobile, it could fire ten penetrating rounds per minute which could pierce 120 mm armor from 900m.

The Achilles was issued to Polish armored units as well as British divisions. The M10 was also issued and was know as the Wolverine by the British. The Achilles was popular with the Anti-Tank regiments of the Royal Artillery.

THE 'PRIEST' AND 'SEXTON' SELF-PROPELLED GUNS

These mobile howitzers were built on the M4 Sherman chassis and the Grizzly chassis respectively. They were designed to provide artillery support to infantry units.

This 25-pounder Sexton is passing through the ruins of Écouché in August 1944. The Sexton was the Canadian equivalent of the M7 Priest.

*Above: this signals lamp formed just a part of the mass of equipment kept onboard armored vehicles.
(Van Onsem Collection)*

....

Opposite: this view of a Sexton reveals the key difference between this vehicle and a Priest.

....

*Following page: these Priests have their guns pointing skywards. In action, the second gunner rammed home the shells into the open breach of the gun using his closed fist.
(National Archives)*

The Priest was fitted with a 105 mm howitzer in a particularly unusual way, right down the central axis of the vehicle. To its right was positioned a machine-gun cupola, raised like a kind of pulpit. This might explain the Priest nickname bestowed on the vehicle by the British. Certain versions had permanent reserve fuel tanks fitted as part of the vehicle's structure. The armor plating to the fore of the vehicle could be raised or lowered. The driver's forward vision was through a hatch cut in the armor plating as well as a protoscope which could be covered in bad weather with a windshield. The vehicle was open on top and the engine was designed so that it could keep up with the most mobile armored vehicles.

The M7 was a sound piece of equipment combining firepower with good protective armor. It met with considerable success and was used in great numbers by Allied forces. Some were converted to radio vehicles, guaranteeing communication between vehicles or pinpointing targets for other Priests.

The Priest carried three types of ammunition: high explosive, anti-tank (the M67 HEAT), explosive (the M1 HE) and smoke (the M84 Smoke). There were 24 in each heavy-armor division's artillery battalion. The M7 chassis was the basis for a transport variant used by the British and Canadians - the Unfrocked Priest, extrapolated from the Kangaroo.

Just as with the priest Sextons received their orders via field telephone or via radio. (Illustration by Jean Restayn)

TECHNICAL DATA

(Sexton)

Crew: 6

Combat weight: 25.8 tons

Engine: Continental R-975, 9-cylinder gasoline engine, 400 hp

Max. speed on road: 40 km/h

Max. speed across country: 32 km/h

Range on road: 230 km

Length: 6.12 m

Width: 2.71 m

Height: 2.43 m

Armament: 1 x 25-pounder Mk II howitzer, 2 x 7.92 mm Bren machineguns

Ammunition: 112 shells, 150 rounds

Armor thickness (max.): 25 mm

Although the vehicle performed satisfactorily, it was problematic as far as the British were concerned, because of its 105 mm gun. Due to difficult supply conditions, there was a shortage of 105 mm shells. In order therefore to correct this problem, the British produced a variant mounting a 25-pounder gun on a Canadian Grizzly chassis. Known as the Sexton it was distinguished by its open-topped fighting compartment, a unique driving sprocket and distinctive tracks. In many respects it looked like the Priest but as the driver was placed on the right the gun was shifted over to the left.

There were three mounts installed for the positioning of Bren guns. In order to maximize the gun's elevation steps had to be taken to minimize its recoil. The vehicle carried 112 shells and had a crew of six.

The Sexton was so successful that it largely replaced the Priest; indeed, by the end of the Normandy campaign, the Priest had almost disappeared although a few were converted into command vehicles.

THE UNIVERSAL CARRIER AND THE 'KANGAROO' APC

The Universal Carrier was designed to carry a machine gun, ammunition and a crew of three. This tracked vehicle, an integral part of a mechanized unit, was popular and used en masse throughout the British and Commonwealth forces.

This Universal Carrier belongs to a machine-gun section of the 1st Battalion of the Podhale Chasseurs, part of the 1st Polish Armoured Division. They have been photographed on August 9, 1944, during Operation Totalize. (Tank Museum 1423/A4)

Below: a steel helmet (Helmet, Steel, RAC Mark I) as worn by tank crews. Such equipment was worn by men of the RAC, by reconnaissance units and by Headquarters Liaison regiments. (Militaria Magazine)

There were two main variants - the Bren Carrier, designed to carry a Bren which evolved into the Vickers Universal Carrier, and the troop transporter, which was also used to tow the 6-pounder, built by Lloyd. There were other lesser versions for example, the Scout carrier, identical to the Bren Carrier but carrying a radio transmitter and receiver.

The Universal Carrier, destined to replace the Bren Carrier and Scout Carrier, offered improved protection. Its main armament consisted of an automatic Bren gun or a Boys anti-tank rifle. In Normandy the Universal Carrier was employed most frequently as an artillery towing unit, sometimes mounting a mortar.

Another vehicle designed to transport troops emerged during the Normandy campaign. The Kangaroo Armoured Personnel Carrier, with its improvised armor, was used to transport infantry and allow them to keep up with armored units.

The Kangaroo provided them with mobility and a measure of protection. Initially, the vehicle used a Priest

TECHNICAL DATA

(Universal Carrier)

Crew: 3
Combat weight: 4.3 tons
Engine: Ford V8 GAU
Mercury, 8-cylinder gasoline
engine, 85 hp
Max. speed on road:
48 km/h
Width: 2.10 m
Height: 1.60 m
Armament: 1 x 7.92 mm
Bren machinegun
Armor thickness (max.):
10 mm
Radio: No. 11

*O*pposite: a Ram Kangaroo belonging to the 79th Armoured Division. The Ram chassis resembled in many ways the Canadian Grizzly chassis. (IWM)

....

*P*receding page: a Bren carrier of the 1st Motor Battalion of the Grenadier Guards (Guards Armoured Division) crosses the Orne during Operation Goodwood. (IWM)

A Universal Carrier. The carrier belonged to a family of tracked vehicles used almost exclusively by Commonwealth forces.
They could also carry ammunition as the 75 mm shell, used by British Sherman, shown on previous page.
(Illustration by Jean Restayn)

chassis and some 72 Priests were modified in August 1944 by the removal of the howitzer, its cradle and the ammunition storage capacity. The Kangaroo Priest could carry 10 infantrymen and their equipment as well as 2 crewmembers.

Later, Canadian Ram chassis that were available in large numbers replaced them. This could carry two crewmen and between 8 and 11 infantrymen.

It also boasted a 12.7 mm machine gun. Most of these served with the 79th Armoured Division.

THE DAIMLER SCOUT CAR 'DINGO' AND THE DAIMLER ARMOURED CAR (Mk I and II)

These two vehicles, the second modeled on the first, were frequently encountered in Normandy. Their widespread use gave them a great reputation.

*T*he Daimler six-cylinder, 2.5 liter gasoline engine gave the Dingo 55hp, which ensured excellent performance.
The crew of two was protected by armor, which varied from 3 mm to 30 mm. (IWM)

The Dingo was a small, angular vehicle some 3 meters long. It was also a great success. Its cross-country qualities (it had independent suspension for each wheel), its robustness, flexibility, speed (88 km/h), mechanical reliability and ease of upkeep placed it in a class apart and made it extremely popular. Because of its role as a reconnaissance or liaison vehicle, it was lightly-armed with just a Bren gun sometimes reinforced by an anti-aircraft machinegun, limiting its usefulness in combat. But it did perform other functions. It worked as an auxiliary vehicle in mine-clearing missions or acted as transport for superior officers.

It was in service in practically all of the British and Commonwealth forces and was also employed by armored and mechanized units. The Armoured Car Mark I was derived from the Dingo and, like it, was conceived as a light tank on wheels.

It was a very versatile vehicle, combining excellent reliability with speed. The engine was designed in 1941 and had a five-speed preselector gearbox, but there were other innovations too with independent suspension, disk breaks and a hydraulic clutch. This four-wheel drive vehicle was particularly adept at crossing rough terrain, while a second steering wheel at the back allowed the vehicle a quick escape. The Armoured Car had a Tetrach's turret mounting a 40 mm gun and a 7.92 mm machinegun.

*A*British manual for recognizing German turreted armor.
(J. Bouchery Collection)

*O*pposite:
one of the characteristics of the Dingo was the large chest, used for storing equipment, on the front of the vehicle.
It had a range of 322 km.
(IWM)

The Daimler Scout Car had a distinctive look due to its angular shape, its superstructure, the storage chest and the very long engine cowling. (Illustration by Jean Restayn)

TECHNICAL DATA
(Scout Car Daimler)
Crew: 2
Combat weight: 3 tons
Engine: Daimler, 6-cylinder gasoline engine, 55 hp
Max. speed on road: 88 km/h
Range on road: 322 km
Length: 3.22 m
Width: 1.70 m
Height: 1.50 m
Armament: 1 or 2 x 7.92 mm Bren machineguns
Armor thickness (max.): 30 mm

The obsolete gun suffered from one particular fault - it could not fire penetrating rounds, making it unsuitable for infantry support. Some vehicles were adapted significantly in order to boost the vehicle's speed and in 1944 the turret, which was of little use anyway, was removed.

The Armoured Car, along with the Dingo, was the backbone of mechanized regiments, each being issued with 13 such vehicles.

Top right: sleeve insignia as worn by a 'Phantom' regiment, a communications unit grouped under the auspices of the No. 1 GHQ Liaison Regiment in Normandy. The Dingo was one of their favorite vehicles. (Militaria Magazine)

....

Opposite: the turret used by the Daimler Armoured Car Mark I was so small that it did not allow the installation of a gun any more powerful than the 2-pounder cannon. (IWM)

THE ARMOURED CAR AEC MARK II AND III, WHITE M3A1

The angular shape of the Armoured Car AEC Mark III, along with its sheer height, is apparent in this photograph. (Bovington Tank Museum)

Headphones for use with a Tannoy. (Van Onsem Collection)

The Armoured Car AEC Mark II (and III) was born from experience gained in the desert. Conceived as a tank on wheels it was well armored with an electrically operated turret and, for the type of vehicle, a relatively powerful 57 mm anti-tank gun.

Its broad chassis was derived from the one used by the Matador tank-towing vehicle but largely modified. The front of the vehicle was sloped but the rest, like the turret, was relatively rectangular. The Mark III carried a 6-pounder or 75 mm gun, the British equivalent of the American M3, and its firepower meant that it was retained in service until the end of the war. Of the vehicle's four wheels, two could be disengaged whilst traveling on road. The vehicle gave good service but was one of the vehicles, like the Morris Mark II Car Light Reconnaissance, which saw little action in Normandy, where the Staghound was more frequently encountered. Nevertheless a few heavy armor regiments used them although they represented only 8 out of 67 armored vehicles in an Armoured Car Regiment. The White M3A1 Scout Car was an

Very few AECs were actually employed in Normandy. The role that they were initially designed for was gradually taken over by the Staghound Armoured Car. (Illustration by Jean Restayn)

TECHNICAL DATA

(AEC Armoured Car Mark II)

Crew: 4
Combat weight: 12.7 tons
Engine: AEC, 6-cylinder diesel engine, 155 hp
Max. speed on road: 66 km/h
Range on road: 402 km
Length: 5.18 m
Width: 2.70 m
Height: 2.70 m
Armament: 1 x 6-pounder (57 mm) gun, 1 x 7.92 mm Besa machinegun
Radio: No. 19

all-terrain vehicle suitable as a command vehicle, reconnaissance vehicle or one which could act as an artillery observation vehicle. It should not be confused with the M5/M9 International Harvester half-track supplied to the British by the Americans. This latter vehicle was also used to transport infantry, allowing them to keep up with the tanks and it was the rival of the German Spw 251. Some of the Whites had front-wheel drive to enable them to cross ditches and not sink into boggy ground. Others were fitted with towing gear to haul stranded vehicles.

Opposite: the American White M3A1 Scout Car had been used by the British since 1941. The M3 half-track had largely replaced it by 1944 but the British still continued to use it until the end of the war. (IWM)

Above: British Army paraffin safety lantern. (Van Onsem Collection)

THE T17 ARMOURED CAR 'STAGHOUND'

This large American armored vehicle was also designed for desert warfare but was not actually employed by the US Army. Modified by the British, it began to replace Daimler vehicles in reconnaissance squadrons and at HQs.

A superb frontal shot of a Staghound just emerging from the factory. A total of 2,844 vehicles were manufactured, mainly delivered to Great Britain, Canada and New Zealand. (National Archives)

B elow: goggles as supplied to tank crews, drivers and motorcyclists. (Militaria Magazine)

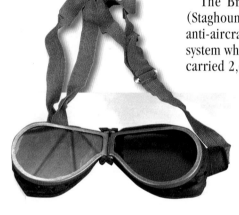

Its most distinguishing feature was its twin 97-horse power engines, which could operate together or independently, each with their own hydramatic transmissions. The vehicles were sturdy, reliable and fast. Its range could be further increased by the addition of supplementary fuel tanks fitted to each flank. The turret, which rotated by means of an electro-hydraulic system, was sloped at 45 degrees and was equipped with a 37 mm gun along with two 7.62 mm machineguns.

The Staghound was most frequently found in armored car regiments. It was relatively common in Normandy but never really became very popular, because it was considered too wide and too heavy for service in Europe.

The British developed an anti-aircraft variant, the T17 E2 (Staghound AA) with a Frazer Nash turret armed with two 12.7 mm anti-aircraft machineguns controlled by a unique electro-hydraulic system which could rotate each gun 60 degrees a second. Each gun carried 2,610 rounds.

B elow: Staghounds in Normandy. The additional fuel tanks were rarely used during active service. (IWM)

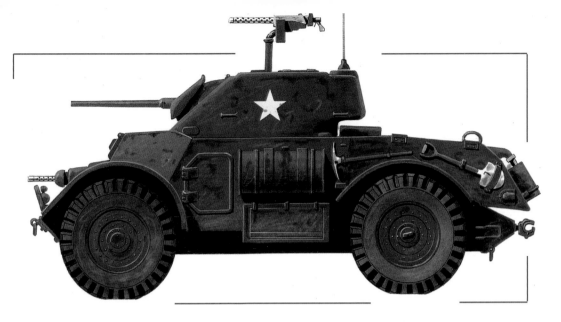

TECHNICAL DATA

Crew: 5
Combat weight: 14.5 tons
Engine: 2 x GMC 270s,
6-cylinder diesel engines,
97 hp
Max. speed on road:
89 km/h
**Range on road (with
reserve tanks):** 724 km
Length: 5.6 m
Width: 2.6 m
Height: 2.31 m
Armament: 1 x 37 mm M6,
2 x 12.7 mm M1919 A4 Brow-
ning machineguns, and 2 x
50.8 mm grenade launchers
Ammunition: 103 shells,
5,250 rounds
Armor thickness (max.):
38 mm
Radio: No. 19

*T*op right: an oil can as used by
the crew of a Staghound.
(Van Onsem Collection)

....

*O*pposite: the Staghound's
turret was operated by
electro-hydraulic controls but
aiming the gun was manual.
(IWM B9421)

*T*he Staghound armored car was initially developed for escort
and reconnaissance duties. *(Illustration by Jean Restayn)*

The radio, a No. 19 wireless, was placed in the turret, because of the lack of interior space. Nearly
1,000 vehicles were eventually produced before
manufacture ceased in
April 1944. The vehi-
cle saw service among
anti-aircraft platoons, part of armored car regiments. Some served as command vehicles, being known as Staghound
Command, and these had their turrets removed. A few other armored
cars also saw service in Normandy but in relatively small numbers.

THE HUMBER MARK IV ARMOURED CAR AND SCOUT CAR

The Humber Mark IV accounted for a large proportion of all British armored car production.

The Humber Mark IV Armoured Car was based on the chassis of the KT4 artillery tractor. The six-cylinder motor was in the rear of the vehicle. The hull was identical to that of the Guy Mark IA armored car with some further modifications. The glacis had a distinct slope and the rear radiator was protected by the addition of a large bulkhead. The turret was redesigned, making it more spacious, and it was equipped with a 37 mm American gun as well as a 7.92 mm Besa machine gun. The vehicle carried a crew of four and the driver could open an aperture in the rear bulkhead for greater visibility behind the vehicle, by means of a special lever.

The vehicle saw a lot of service in a variety of theaters, and was predominantly used to equip reconnaissance units attached to infantry divisions. Another version, the Humber AA Mark I, was also utilized. This was designed as an anti-aircraft vehicle with four 7.92 mm Besa machineguns.

This lightly armored Humber Scout Car carries the insignia and markings of the 5th Royal Tank Regiment (11th Armoured Division). (Illustration by Jean Restayn)

TECHNICAL DATA
(Scout Car Humber)

Crew: 2 or 3
Combat weight: 3.9 tons
Engine: Humber 26, 6-cylinder gasoline engine, 88 hp
Max. speed on road: 100 km/h
Range on road: 320 km
Length: 3.83 m
Width: 1.89 m
Height: 2.10 m
Armament: 1 x 7.92 mm Bren machinegun
Armor thickness (max.): 14 mm
Radio: No. 19

Right: a box containing the control unit of a wireless set No. 19. (Van Onsem Collection)

Opposite: the asymmetric structure of a Humber Scout Car is clearly shown in this photograph. The floor of the vehicle was so thin that it offered virtually no protection against mines. (Tank Museum 455/C4)

The Humber Scout Car, wider than its Daimler counterpart, could accommodate a crew of three and had modified hatches so that a remote-controlled Bren gun could be mounted on runners. The transverse suspension had semi-elliptical springs.

The vehicle was used throughout the war by Commonwealth forces, particularly in tank or armored car units.

PRACTICAL INFORMATION

This information focuses on places which saw armored combat or where substantial numbers of tanks played a part in the battle for Normandy. Military-vehicle enthusiasts should note that we list places where actual vehicles can be seen as well bigger museums and commemorative monuments.

CALVADOS

At Port-en-Bessin there is a **unique museum** of underwater artefacts. It is unique in that it presents items dredged up from the sea-bed: tanks, trucks and other vehicles. It's a novel way of rendering homage to the liberators.

Musée des épaves sous-marines du débarquement
Route de Bayeux – BP Commes
14520 Port-en-Bessin
Tel: 02 31 21 17 06

Open everyday from June to 30 September. Open weekends in May, 10.00 to 12.00 and 14.00 to 18.00.

Also worth a visit: three plaques and two steles

Some five miles to the south is Bayeux with its **Battle of Normandy Memorial Museum**. It evokes the 77 days of the campaign, has three galleries and covers a large area. Around a hundred uniforms are on display as well as a **Sherman tank**, an **M10 Tank Destroyer**, a **Churchill** and a **Hetzer** (an interesting vehicle which, however, was not deployed in Normandy). There's also a cinema (150 seat-cinema) showing short films on the campaign.

Musée-Mémorial de la Bataille de Normandie
Boulevard Fabian Ware - BP 21215
14402 Bayeux CEDEX
Tél.: 02 31 92 93 41 - fax: 02 31 21 85 11
www.mairie-bayeux.fr.

Open all year. From 17 September to 30 April, 10.00 to 12.30 and 14.00 to 18.00. From 1 May to 16 September, 09.30 to 18.30. Closed in the second half of January.

Also worth a visit: general de Gaulle's Museum, British Cemetery, monuments, steles and plaques.

From Bayeux head west to Saint-Laurent-sur-Mer. There, not far from Omaha Beach, and close by the American cemetery at Colleville, is the **Omaha Beach Memorial Museum**. Apart from countless artefacts, uniforms and weapons from D-day there are also important records relating to the Resistance and Deportation and details of the economic plight of the region under the Germans. An excellent panorama recreates the landings whilst a **Sherman** and a **155 mm Long Tom** can be seen in the car park as well as a **landing craft**.

Musée d'Omaha Beach à Saint-Laurent-sur-Mer
« Les moulins » - rue de la mer
14710 Saint-Laurent-sur-Mer
Tél.: 02 31 21 97 44 - fax: 02 31 92 72 80
http://www.museememorial-omaha. com

Open from 15 February to 15 March (10.00 to 12.30 and 14.30 to 18.00), 16 March to 15 May (9.30 to 18.30), 16 May to 15 September (09.30 to 19.00 except July-August: 9.30 to 19.30) and from 15 September to 15 November (9.30 to 18.30).

The American cemetery at Saint Laurent/Colleville might also be of interest with its commemorative plaques and monuments.

From Bayeux you can also head east. Five miles to the north-east is the **Arromanches Museum**, built by the site of the Mulberry harbour. There's a **half-track**, a **Sherman** and **two artillery guns**. The diorama, models, films and exhibits cover the whole of Overlord.

Musée du débarquement d'Arromanches
Place du 6 juin
14117 Arromanches
Tél.: 02 31 22 34 31 - fax: 02 31 92 68 83
www.normandy1944.com

Open all year round (except January): from 10.00 to 12.30 and 13.30 to 17.00. In summer opening hours are 09.00 to 19.00.

The **360° museum at Arromanches** is also of interest.

Five miles to the east of Arromanches in the centre of Ver-sur-Mer, by the D 514, is a **British Sexton**. The museum of the **America-Gold Beach** is also here. There are two buildings and exhibits describe the landings as well as the role of the 50th Division in King sector, Gold Beach.

Musée America-Gold Beach
2, place Amiral Byrd
14114 Ver-sur-Mer
Tél. fax: 02 31 22 58 58

Opening hours:
From 10.30 to 13.30 and 14.30 to 17.30 in July and August.
Wednesdays and Thursdays (09.30 to 12.00) from 1 November to 30 April. Closed Tuesdays in May, June, September and October.

Also worth a visit: two monuments, two plaques and a board.

Again to the east is Courseulles-sur-Mer with its **monument to the Royal Winnipeg Rifles** and, close to the sea front, a **Sherman tank** restored in 1970. There are also a number of plaques and monuments in the town. In the adjoining town of Graye-sur-Mer there is a **British Churchill mortar** tank near the Liberation monument.

Six miles from Courseulles, at Lion-sur-Mer, there is a **Churchill AVRE** at the western exit of the town on the D 514. In the neighboring town of Hermanville-sur-Mer, and again by the D 514, there is a **British Centaur** and the **British cemetery** with its 1,005 graves and four monuments.

Not far from the beach at Ouistreham, is the **Atlantic Wall Museum**. This is located in a vast bunker, the former HQ commanding all the batteries along the Orne estuary. It gives the visitor a real insight into the way such defences functioned. The rooms are on five levels and have been fitted out just as they were. There are boiler rooms, sleeping quarters, a pharmacy, a hospital, magazines, communication rooms and an observation post fitted with a powerful range-finder.

Musée du bunker du Mur de l'Atlantique
Boulevard du 6 juin
14150 Ouistreham-Riva-Bella
Tél.: 02 31 97 28 69 - fax: 02 31 96 66 05
e. mail: bunkermusée@aol.com

Opening hours:
10.00 to 18.00 from 3 February to 15 November
09.00 to 19.00 from 1 April to 30 September
Closed 16 November to 2 February